Sustainable Play

Mollie Chambers
Early Years and Primary Practitioner
Outdoor Learning Lead
Mummy/manager of three children

Sustainable Play

All rights reserved. No part of this publication may be reproduced, stored in a retrieval system, or transmitted, in any form or by any means, electronic, mechanical, photocopying, recording or otherwise, without the prior written permission of the author.

Copyright © Mollie Chambers 2022

Please note that some of the activities contained within this book carry risk. Any reader or anyone in their charge taking part in any of the activities described does so at their own risk. Neither the author nor the publisher can accept any legal responsibility for any harm, injury, damage, loss or prosecution resulting from the use or misuse of the activities, techniques, tools and advice in this book.

Contents

Introduction	7
What is sustainable play?	9
Why is sustainable play important?	13
Sustainable toys	17
Sustainable art and craft	21
Sustainable sensory	41
Natural resource play	55
Food play	71
Natural environment play	91
Zero waste play	107
Final thoughts	120
Recipes	121-7
Shopping list essentials	128

INTRODUCTION

If you're anything like me, it's likely you're exhausted from the effort involved in making environmentally conscious choices in a world that simply isn't ready. I find myself worrying about the impact of play, food shopping and resources on the environment. I want to teach my children not to be wasteful, to reuse and focus on having fun rather than consuming. The difficulty is, when I pull apart a 'sustainable' activity, think carefully about the resourcing and the potential waste, I often discover that the activity is not at all sustainable. So I've created this book to ease the head spinning and give you examples of activities that really are one hundred per cent sustainable. My activities are always low resource, low input and high output. You should be able to grab the resources from your creative area, kitchen or from the natural environment. I have included 'shopping list essentials' at the back of this book but, as always, the most sustainable play involves using what you already have.

Good luck!

Mollie

What is sustainable play?

What is sustainable play?

If we first consider the word 'sustainability' it helps us to put into context what sustainable play might look like. The meaning of the word 'sustainability' is, avoidance of the depletion of natural resources. In an ideal world our children would play and have no impact on the environment but I think that would be exceptionally difficult to do. The benchmark for me is that the *majority* of my children's play is low impact or no impact. I've had to accept that my crafty eldest son likes using a glue gun, despite every effort, my daughter likes plastic dolls and my youngest son likes to display his coin collection in plastic wallets. We can't do everything perfectly but as you become more conscious and analytical of the activities your child engages in, you will begin to see how little adaptations can lessen the impact. So for me 'sustainable play' is not about perfect play but about adapting play so the impact is as small as you can make it. Therefore, my daughter plays with pre-loved dolls, I've taught my eldest how to attach parts together without the need for glue (more on that later) and my youngest only displays his favourite coins (the remaining coins are stored in a box). Sustainable play for us is about reusing rather than consuming, playing and connecting with the natural environment and having an awareness of resources as we use them. As you read on you will learn how to reduce the impact of your child's play and how to provide opportunities for zero waste play.

Why is it important to provide opportunities for sustainable play?

Why is it important to provide opportunities for sustainable play?

My favourite phrase is 'the best lessons involve action'. I believe this is true for most learners; young and old. To help children understand concepts you have to give them 'real' opportunities to learn. We can teach our children how a plant grows and look in books or online but the most effective way for them to learn is to experience it for themselves. The learning is deeper because when you plant a seed, give it water and sunlight it doesn't always grow. Your child will see that some, not all, of the seeds they put in the ground will develop into plants. They'll witness insects and animals eating what they've grown as well as the effects of extreme weather. These are real and memorable learning experiences that stay with children so when your child plays sustainably it helps them to learn about sustainability. As well as this, I use 'sustainability talk' to help my children understand how the materials they use and the products they buy can impact the environment. They have an acute understanding of the harms that single use plastics are having on the ocean and land and they actively avoid buying products made of plastic (my twins are five and my eldest is seven). By playing sustainably and talking about how the play is sustainable we are giving our children the tools needed to make sustainable choices as future consumers. During their early years, children are sponges, they soak up information at an incredible rate. They are formulating their ideas and opinions and we mustn't underestimate the influence we have on them. Sustainable play is about love, respecting the resources that come from the planet and considering the impacts of our actions. These are beautiful lessons so let's teach them…

Sustainable Toys

Sustainable Toys

If you've been inside a toyshop recently you may have noticed that most of the products designed for children are made of plastic. Plastic is bright and children are naturally attracted to bright colours but the resources you give your child do not need to be as over stimulating as possible. The real reason for the lights, sounds, colours and packaging is that toy manufacturers are in competition. The are not producing products that children *need* they are producing products that children will want, beg and pester for. This is not to say that my home is free from plastic toys. We have pre-loved construction bricks and the occasional gift has made its way in but the vast majority of my children's toys are sustainable (the key to this is not to have too many). It's very difficult to bring up children and avoid plastic completely but if you buy pre-loved and make sure that most of your toys are paper or wood based, you're doing a fantastic job. Away from the toyshop shelves you will be able to find many more sustainable options. Online retailers are flying flag right now so take a look online and you'll find some wonderful, sustainably sourced toys. Don't assume wood, paper and cardboard resources are automatically sustainable. Check the labelling carefully for things like 'FSC'; I can guarantee that if a product is sustainable the manufacturer will label it as such. If you want some examples of sustainable toys that will support physical development and grow with your child read 'Tool Play'. As a general rule I would avoid toys that are limited to a developmental stage lasting six months and try to find toys that can be played with across a range of developmental stages. If you couple your toy play with outdoor play, sensory play, creative play and zero waste play you can be sure that you are achieving a good balance of everything.

Sustainable Art and Craft

Sustainable Art and Craft

I would describe my relationship with art and craft as 'love, hate'. On one hand, engagement in art and craft allows my children to express themselves, be creative, independent and develop physically. The downside is, if you're not careful, you can create a huge amount of waste or end up with piles of artwork and a cardboard craft museum in your spare room (or wherever you decide to hide it). When your child creates something, they might use glue, sticky tape or decoration, instantly making the recyclable, unrecyclable. If we haven't got the time to carefully pull their creation apart (which we usually haven't) the whole lot might end up in the bin, in landfill or up in flames at the local incinerator. The solution to this is not to avoid art and craft but to explore ways to reduce the impact of it; there are lots of ways to do this. Don't feel guilty if your child creates something out of cardboard, stuck together with PVA and painted with a thick coat of acrylic paint but make sure that you provide some low waste art and craft activities too.

Compostable art and Craft

This is my absolute 'art and craft' love. Create, enjoy and compost it. Zero waste, art and craft for your child and food for the garden; it doesn't get more sustainable than that. Play is not about the having lots of expensive resources but finding an outlet for your child's creativity that has a low environmental impact.

Play-Ready
Newspaper is compostable; in fact most paper is but check carefully before composting paper. If it has glitter, foil or a coating the only place it can go is the bin.

Five quick ideas
Eggshell mosaic: Always save your eggshells. It only takes a second to wash them out and have a cardboard box to put them in. When you have time (or get your child to do it) break the shells into pieces, separate them into piles and colour them with food colouring. Now you have your very own compostable mosaic pieces. Use natural adhesive (20g flour and 35ml water) to stick the pieces on newspaper. Enjoy the artwork then compost it.

Compostable crowns: Use newspaper and natural adhesive. If you want colour, collect some flowers, make slits and poke the stems through. Play and compost.

Paper Mache: Use the same natural adhesive to make your paper Mache. Ideally you want to avoid using a balloon so use tinfoil over a bowl or cup depending on what size you want your creation to be. As long as you decorate it with natural resources and compostable paint you can compost the whole thing, as and when your child has finished using it (or while they're out of the house).

Rice art: You can make some temporary art with rice in a tray or glue coloured rice to compostable paper. As long as you use natural adhesive it's fine to compost.

Natural resource art: Any artwork made with flowers, seeds, leaves or any compostable materials can be disposed of in your compost heap. Obviously you don't want your compost to be filled to the top with paper so make sure your child's creative development has a good balance of compostable, temporary, food, recyclable and low waste art. If they create the occasional glue gunned acrylic nightmare don't beat yourself up.

Painting

Did you know that as soon as your child puts brush to paper the paper becomes non-recyclable? Painting feels likes an eco-friendly activity because you are using paper and not plastic but if you always use acrylic paint you will find your child produces a lot of waste.

Play-Ready
Have a stock of chalk and use brightly coloured vegetable peel or fruit to make paint. Think about your local area and whether there are any opportunities for natural resource painting.

Five quick ideas
Vegetable paint: Bright vegetables such as beetroot, carrot, red cabbage and spinach are perfect for paint. Use up vegetable peel or old vegetables that aren't fresh enough to eat.

Berry paint: Berries are fantastic for paint. Raspberries, blueberries and blackberries give a really strong colour. If you have some leftover berries that are about to turn use them for painting. Paint on paper and you can dispose of it by composting it.

Temporary painting: not every painting needs to be hung on the wall or stored inside an art book. Provide a mix of permanent, compostable and temporary art activities and this will have a huge impact on the waste your child's creative development produces. If you have paving slabs outside and some old pieces of chalk you can make paint that washing away in the rain. Crush up the chalk, mix with water (your child can help) and provide brushes. They can paint and then wash it off or let the rain do the work.

Mud painting: Another way to create some temporary art is to use mud. Either at home on the paving slabs or on a wall outside. If you're in the woods it can be done on a tree or large leaf.

Charcoal painting: As with chalk, crush the charcoal in a bowl and mix with a little water. Use brushes to paint on paving slabs or paper.

Printing

Where painted paper cannot be recycled, inked paper can. So rather than always planning for paper and paint artwork make sure you plan for printing, painting using natural resources and temporary painting and mark making. If you have a good mix of these activities it will reduce the environmental impact and your child will actually be engaging in a broader variety of creative play; win, win.

Play-Ready
Have a set of wooden stampers and ink in your creative area.

Five quick ideas
Wrapping paper: Use stampers to decorate a piece of paper to wrap a present. Most wrapping paper cannot be recycled so this has triple impact: creative development, playing for purpose and creating recyclable wrap.

Finger printing: Very messy but if you have an ink pad at home your child can use it make finger print pictures. The prints could be leaves on a tree, animals or rainbows.

Border paper: Use ink stampers to create beautiful paper with a boarder. If your child is able to write they could use the paper to write a recipe, letter, story or poem.

Greetings card: Use ink instead of paint to make a special card for a friend or loved one. They can recycle it afterwards.

Lolly stick puppets: Use inked characters on paper attached to lolly sticks and have your own puppet show. When your child has finished with the puppets, remove, recycle the paper and reuse the sticks.

Natural Art and craft

An incredibly sustainable way to engage in art and craft activities is to use natural resources. Not gluing natural resources together with PVA and glue guns or painting them with acrylic. Think about how you can assemble resources together without gluing and how to use nature's colours instead of painting.

Play-Ready
Use the natural resources that you have collected on walks.

Five quick ideas
Fairy crowns: Make a band with a piece of paper and cut slits along it. Encourage your child to collect flowers and poke them through the slits to make a beautiful crown.

Wreath: This time use a card circle with slits or small holes. Collect seasonal foliage and decorate.

Magic wands: Collect sticks while out walking; use natural twine or long grass to tie sticks and leaves to your wand.

Fairy/safari houses: Collect natural resources and assemble them to make fairy houses or safari houses for wild animals.

Castles: Design and create castles on the beach or in a sandpit. Use natural resources to decorate or if you're on the beach and want to raise awareness, collect manmade materials and decorate with those.

Woodland mobile: find a medium sized stick and tie four or five pieces of string to it. Collect natural resources while walking and tie them to the stick. You could focus on colour, texture or scent and theme your mobile.

Woodwork

Woodwork seems like a very child-un-friendly activity but it doesn't need to involve large-scale construction and complicated tasks. Your young child might not be ready for tools yet but you can still plan for woodwork using pre-cut wood and assemble/decorate-style activities.

Play-Ready
If your child is older or more able you might have already introduced them to tools, they might have their own tool box or use your tools. For a younger child you might provide wooden lolly sticks, pre-cut wooden shapes or pieces of wood to assemble.

Five quick ideas
Wooden robots: This is great starter activity that you can either prep or if your child is more able, they can do the prep. You need two cubes of wood, one for the head and one for the body. Make four holes and use large screws for the arms and legs. Use a double-ended screw to attach the head to the body and use ink pens to draw the detail.

Lolly stick raft: Use lolly sticks and string to make a raft. Test it in the bath or in a stream.

Number tiles: Cut slices of wood and your child can write their numbers to ten and a representation of the number in dots on the back. They can use their number tiles for addition, subtraction and ordering. Children always engage more with resources they've created themselves.

Hedgehog: If you have an old door wedge your child can practise hammering small nails into the back of it to make a hedgehog (always supervise).

Wooden boat: Cut a branch into slices. Partially drill a hole into one of the slices and push a small stick in. Make a sail out of a small piece of paper and attach it to your stick mast.

For more in-depth ideas on woodwork and risk assessment read 'Tool Play'.

Fabric

The fashion industry is one of the planet's top polluters. It is estimated that ten per cent of all greenhouse gasses are produced by the fashion industry so we must consume less, reuse more, recycle fabric and if you have an item of clothing that's falling apart, add it to your creative area.

Play-Ready
When you go through old clothes put aside a couple of pieces that could be used for fabric play.

Five quick ideas
Pendants: Cut a piece of card into the shape you want such as a love heart, star or diamond. Cover it with an old scrap of fabric to brighten it up.

Hair bands: Strips of fabric are perfect for repurposing into hair bands. Just fold and tie.

Lolly stick decoration: Take a lolly stick and some strips of fabric. Start at the top of the stick and tie each piece from top to bottom. Green fabric is perfect for a Christmas tree decoration.

Bookmark: Reuse an old piece of fabric by sticking it to card to make a bookmark.

Wreath: Use the same method you used with the lolly stick and tie each piece of fabric to your card circle until it's covered.

Recyclable Craft

I'm all about making sure the recyclable stays recyclable (as much as possible) so this is not about reusing and then binning what your child has made (that feels sustainable but it's actually really wasteful). There's definitely a time and place for glitter and glue but it's not *all* the time.

Play-Ready
Create an area for things like tubes and cardboard. Allow access to these and explore way to attach resources together without glue.

Five quick ideas
Tying: This is a fantastic way to temporarily attach resources together. When your child has finished using what they have made you can cut the twine, reuse or compost it (if it's natural) and recycle the cardboard.

Slotting: You can build houses, trees, stars, and all sorts of three-dimensional objects by cutting a slice in each part and slotting them together. When it's time for the recycling bin you can simply pull your child's project apart and recycle it.

Building: This can be a temporary project. If you have lots of cardboard boxes and tubes your child can build with them. There's no need to glue or paint anything and you can dismantle it when they've finished, use the boxes for craft and then recycle them. This way you really have maximised the potential of the resource.

Small amounts of glue: A glue stick can be used to join cardboard parts together and as long as your child has only used small amounts, the cardboard can still be recycled.

Decorating: As I mentioned earlier, if your child paints their project it can't be recycled. Use ink for decoration; felt tips and inkpads are fine to use on cardboard. If your child wants bright colours, you could use coloured paper with small amounts of glue and the whole thing can be recycled. Check your paper carefully because glitter, coated, foiled and shiny paper cannot be recycled. They look beautiful but you have to consider whether it's worth it for the waste. I would suggest only using these types of paper every now and again or try to live without them. If your child is desperate for glitter, use biodegradable glitter on compostable art.

Temporary Art

A wonderful way to engage in art and achieve zero waste play is to create temporary art. Your child can create something amazing, you can take a picture as a record and leave the work where it is.

Play-Ready
Simple plan for time outside or use the colourful resources inside your home.

Five quick ideas
Flora and fawner rainbow: Collect colourful flowers, leaves and plants. Make a temporary rainbow on the ground.

Pebble art: find as many shapes, sizes and colours as possible. Group them as though you're creating a pebble palette and then encourage your child to make some art with them. It could be abstract or something more concrete. Patterns look beautiful on the beach. Work with your child and support as their ideas develop.

Shell art: If you have a beach with lots of sea glass, shells and small natural resources you can make a small piece with these. Sort them as you did with the pebbles and create something beautiful for the tide to take.

Leaves: When I think of leaves I think of colour and shape. You could collect the leaves and take them home to create some temporary art in the garden or make a picture on the forest floor using leaves.

Rainbow: This is perfect for a rainy day. Find things inside the house that are different colours of the rainbow and make a temporary rainbow on the floor.

Sustainable Sensory

Sustainable Sensory

Sensory play is a wonderful way to play sustainably. As with craft, if you're not considerate of your resources it can end up being wasteful but there are a few simple things you can do to cut down on the waste associated with sensory play.

Water

When linking water play and sustainability we must consider the resources that go alongside the play. The water itself is part of the resourcing so if your child's water play involves bath or shower time, a dip in the pool or a play at the beach there is no excess water involved in these activities. If you want to provide extra opportunities for water play, a small tray, the kitchen sink or a mud kitchen is more than enough. Don't get seduced into buying lots of colourful plastic resources because you'll be battling with storage, mould and what to do with them when your child has outgrown them.

Play-Ready

Consider the resources you already have that are waterproof and easy to clean. Create a designated area or think about when and where your child can access water play.

Five quick ideas

Paper boats: Use old newspaper and make an origami boat or create a paper Mache boat.

Water beads and sieves: Always have a stock of water beads. They're extremely tactile and children love playing, sorting and sieving them out of the water.

Shells, pebbles and small world: Collect shells and pebbles during beach walks. Use them with water and small world characters to encourage your child to play creatively.

Frozen play: There are lots way to play with ice. Colour it, hide something inside it, your child can smash it or use salt to melt it quickly.

Citrus: If you have any left over oranges or lemons, cut them into slices and put the slices into a bowl of water for your child to touch, smell and squeeze.

Sand

Like water, there are many places to access sand play without needing to create a designated area. The most sustainable way to access sand is to go to a beach or sand dunes but if you are not a coastal dweller you might be able to find a local park, zoo or activity centre with a sandpit.

Play-Ready
Plan time to visit a sandy area or if you want an area at home, create a little sand tray in your messy play area or outside in your mud kitchen.

Five quick ideas
Sandcastles: On the beach, your child can collect natural resources to decorate or seaweed to strengthen their castle. At home you might have a few natural resources alongside your sand play.

Tubes: Old tubes are fantastic for filling, comparing amounts and making towers of sand. If they get wet just dry them out and recycle them when the play is over.

Loose parts: Loose parts play simply describes play that involves lots of small things. It might be buttons, acorns, pebbles and so on (best for the over threes). Add some loose parts to your sand tray and see how your child interacts with them.

Cookie cutters: Such a versatile tool; cookie cutters work really well with sand play. Your child can cut through the sand with them, print on flattened sand or fill the cutter with loose parts.

Cupcakes: Either lend out your cupcake tray or provide some cupcake cases. Your child can fill them with sand and top with loose parts or natural resources such as flowers for decoration.

Rice

Probably one of the most represented sensory play ideas is a big tuff tray full of brightly coloured rice. Often the rice is immaculately separated into contrasting colours. What you must remember is that once your child has played with the rice it will not look immaculate. It's quite a task colouring rice and not something you want to be doing regularly. If you have storage, colour theme your rice. You might choose different shades of green and a bit of brown mixed in for dinosaur play. If you have fairies and unicorns you might make a rainbow rice to go with that. Once you have created your themes and made a stock of rice you can reuse it again and again. You don't have to worry about colour separation because you've created themes and the colours are already mixed.

Play-Ready

Decide on your themes based on the resources you already have and what your child is interested in. Dye the rice, make sure it is completely dry and store it in jars. For absolute sustainability use refills rather than rice in plastic packaging and store in old jam jars or buy some metal tins.

Five quick ideas

Small world: Have some small world toys alongside your rice for imaginative play.

Containers: Reuse old containers for transporting, measuring, pouring and comparing.

Wooden puzzle board: If you have an old baby puzzle board, take the pieces out and your child can fill the spaces with coloured rice.

Search and find: Hide treasure in the rice. Create a treasure checklist and see if your child can find all the treasure.

Lavender rice: Make sensory rice by adding fragrant flowers. Your child could use a pestle and mortar to crush the flowers and rice together.

Pasta

Pasta comes in all shapes and sizes. It can be dyed and used for threading or sensory play. If you refill your pasta or buy it packaged in paper rather than plastic your activity will be as sustainable as it can be.

Play-Ready
As with rice, create a stock of pasta to reuse each time your child plays.

Five quick ideas
Cooked pasta: Cooked pasta sensory play is great for young children because it's perfectly safe to eat. Cook some spaghetti and let your child touch, taste and smell the warm pasta.

Coloured pasta: Like rice, colour your pasta and keep a stock to reuse. I prefer to do this, rather than cooked because there's less waste involved.

Pasta jewellery: Any pasta that has a hole in it is perfect for threading. You can reuse it, colour it and even gift it. Pasta shaped like animals or themed are a kitchen cupboard must have.

Colander and spaghetti: If, like me you prefer not to use cooked pasta too much, use dry spaghetti and a colander. Your child can poke the spaghetti through the holes. It takes patience and good fine motor control to do this. If the pasta breaks you can still reuse it for sensory play.

Pasta sorting: If your pasta gets in a muddle don't sit there late at night sorting it, get your child to sort it for you. Sorting is part of their mathematical development and pasta is a fun way to cover it.

DOUGH

Another activity that can add to waste is dough play. If you buy a premade dough from the toyshop it usually comes packaged in plastic with lots of plastic accessories. If you don't want to make it, there are companies online that will make natural dough for you. The dough is often packaged in tins or jars rather than plastic tubs and some companies offer sustainable resources with their dough.

Play-Ready
Buy a stock of handmade dough, create a dry mix using the recipe at the back of this book or make your own and store it for your child to use. Most dough, whether shop bought or handmade, will last about six months but the beauty of a natural handmade dough is that you can compost it rather than putting it in the bin.

Five quick ideas
Dough animals: Use natural resources to make dough animals. Leaves for wings, shells for eyes and so on. Your child will love being creative and if you make the dough yourself you can compost it when you're done.

Cupcakes: Use a cupcake tray or cupcake cases. The dough can be the sponge and your child can top their cupcakes with natural resources.

Printing: Printing doesn't always have to be permanent. Paint printing makes the paper unrecyclable whereas dough printing can be done again and again until your dough is ready to be composted. Use cookie cutters, clean ink stampers or cutlery to make temporary patterns on the dough.

Letter and number formation: Roll out the dough into sausage shapes and see if your child can make letters, numbers or, if they're very young, patterns with it.

Sensory dough: You can add all sorts of things to dough to make it more sensory for your child. Essences, dried herbs, flavoured tea, flowers and spices. Lay out a few ingredients and let them explore.

Natural Resource Play

Natural Resource Play

When children interact with natural resources it helps them to build connections with the earth. It encourages them to use their imagination as they play. Natural resource play is one of the most sustainable ways to play.

Pinecones

Pinecones have always been a source of fascination for my children. Perhaps it's the absence of them for months on end until September when the forest floor is littered with them. Perhaps it's some kind of ancestral instinct to gather and collect from the ground. Whatever the reason I think it's important to nurture instinctive behaviour.

Play-Ready
Plan for time outside and always take a bag with you on walks to bring natural resources home. Set up an area inside or out where your child can access natural resources. I tend to keep a little collection of pinecones in my creative area for the children to use.

Five quick ideas
Printing: Use pinecones to print in sand, dough, salt dough or mud.

Painting: Make a natural berry or vegetable paint and use your pinecone as a painting tool.

Pinecone people: Add sticky paper eyes, sticks for arms and old fabric scraps for clothes. Encourage your child to play imaginatively.

Decoration: Pinecones make a beautiful decoration. Add string and biodegradable glitter to use as a Christmas decoration or decorate with dry flowers for an all year round look.

Animals: Add sticky paper eyes and natural resources such as leaves for wings or flowers for fur. Encourage your child to play imaginatively.

Sticks

By the end of every walk at least two of my children will have a stick in their hand. It might become a sword or a walking stick but there are many uses for sticks during play so get collecting.

Play-Ready
If you have a garden with hedges or trees you can take cuttings from these. If you are out walking throw a few sticks in your bag to take home.

Five quick ideas
Stick man: Sticks are a wonderful resource for imaginative play. A stick can transform into any character in your child's imagination. Use paper eyes, fabric squares or simply let your child imagine as they play.

Whittling: Read 'Tool Play' before planning activities that carry risk. If your child has moved up the progression of tools and demonstrates control and coordination you might be able to allow them to use a peeler to strip a stick of its bark. Always supervise. You could use the stick as a magic wand or for the activities on the next page, once it is stripped.

Woodland frame: Introduce tying by making a woodland frame. Find four sticks of similar length (maths opportunity here) and tie them together at each corner. When the frame is complete your child can attach their own artwork, use it to weave or hang flowers from.

Fairy tepee: Find lots of sticks the same length and tie together at the top. Make fairies out of pegs, leaves and flowers.

Stick raft: Find sticks of similar length and tie together. Make a leaf sail and find a stream to test it out.

Shells

If you live near a beach you can find some wonderful treasures to bring home and add to your sustainable play.

Play-Ready
Collect shells of different shapes and sizes. Buy shells if you live inland or ask a friend to collect some for you.

Five quick ideas
Printing: Use shells and natural paint to print. Alternatively use shells to temporary print in dough or sand.

Sorting: If you have a good collection of shells use them for sorting. Encourage your child to choose their own category for sorting. It might be colour, size, shape or texture. If they can't think of a category you can support by making suggestions.

Water play: Create an ocean play scene with small world creatures, shells and coloured water.

Loose parts: Use the shells for loose parts play. Simply provide a good selection of shells and let your child create their own playtime.

Shell necklace: If you have shells with holes, put them to one side for threading. If you have a drill you can easily drill small holes into shells and provide some natural twine to make shell necklaces.

Leaves

Leaves are incredible. A few days ago I was explaining to my daughter that leaves can take the sun's energy and feed the plant with it. She's only five, so I didn't need to go into more detail than that. Needless to say, she was amazed. On a sensory level, leaves provide shape, colour, texture, sound and scent. You'd be hard pushed to find a toy in the toyshop that can stimulate all five senses and have sustainable credentials as well.

Play-Ready

Take cuttings from the garden or collect fallen leaves while walking. Put some fresh and dry leaves in your mud kitchen or dry leaves in your creative area.

Five quick ideas

Sorting: Sort by type, shape, colour or texture. If your child is older you could introduce a Venn diagram into the play.

Crushing: Use a rolling pin and bowl or a pestle and mortar. Dry leaves can be crushed into smaller pieces and used as 'spices' in mud kitchen play and fresh leaves can be crushed with water to make perfume or potions.

Compostable crowns: Fold over a piece of newspaper to make a headband, stick it with natural adhesive (20g flour, 35ml water) leave it to dry. Once dry, cut some small slits along it; these can be used to poke leaves through and your child can wear it as a crown. When they've had enough of it (usually after twenty minutes) you can break it up and compost it.

Temporary art: I love temporary art. We all want to encourage our children's creativity but what we don't want is to create lots of non-recyclable waste in the process. Use leaves to make a beautiful picture on the ground (make sure it's not windy) and take a photo as a record of their work.

Leaf necklace: Use natural twine for this. Collect leaves of different colours and shapes. Tie the leaves onto the twine to make a beautiful leaf necklace. If you use natural twine you can compost the necklace when your child has had enough of it.

Acorns, chestnuts and conkers

Are you familiar with the sound of acorns rolling around your washing machine? My daughter is a master acorn concealer. She will intentionally choose clothes with pockets during autumn so she can collect as many acorns as possible.

Play-Ready
As with all natural resources collect and keep or play with them in the natural environment.

Five quick ideas
Plant: Have a go at growing an oak tree. Plant an acorn and see how it develops. This is a great opportunity for some sustainability talk.

Cook: I wouldn't suggest cooking acorns or conkers but roasted chestnuts are delicious. If your child is older they can help with cutting a little cross in the top and younger children can help with washing the chestnuts.

Sorting: Take a bag with you on autumn walks and collect as much from the ground as you can. Use what you find for a sorting activity.

Printing with acorn cups: A lovely natural way to print with paint or in dough, mud or sand.

Conker snails: Conkers make fabulous shells for snails. Make some natural play dough, roll it into sausage shapes for the body and put a conker on top for the shell.

Pebbles

There's something wonderfully tactile about the feel of a smooth round pebble in your hand. Children love to stack them, arrange them and grind them together.

Play-Ready
Have a small selection of pebbles at home or if you live near a beach allow your child to interact with them in the natural environment.

Five quick ideas
Pebble towers: Use pebbles to stack into towers. Encourage your child to find pebbles of varying sizes and start with the biggest.

Pebble people: I always say that we should never underestimate the power of a child's imagination. I also think that we've created toys, movies and video games that are so real we're losing opportunities for our children to imagine. Create pebble people and your child can engage in imaginative play.

Temporary art: You can make beautiful large-scale mosaic style artwork with pebbles. Either bring some pebbles home or create some artwork on the beach. Your child could even have a go at making their name in pebbles.

Mark making: If you have the luxury of a beach nearby, explore the potential of rocks for mark making. Some rocks can be used to draw on other rocks, charcoal is another option but just use trial and error to see which rock works best.

Shape matching: Draw around each pebble on a piece of paper and your child can match the pebble to its outline:

Food Play

Food Play

When your child interacts with their food it helps them to learn about texture, scent, and colour and gives them time to develop their fine motor control. With three meals and snacks between, there are many opportunities for your child to play sustainably with food. Use it as a play opportunity during the early years.

Snacks

Make it, bake it or buy it, whatever you decide to do, use snack time as an opportunity to play and learn sustainably.

Play-Ready
The way that I feel ready for food play is to make sure I always have a good variety of raw ingredients for baking as well as a range of foods that can be combined without the need for baking.

Five quick no-cook ideas
Rainbow popcorn: Colour some popcorn and your child can make a rainbow to help them learn about the seven colours or they could thread the popcorn with cereal hoops to make an edible necklace.

Fruit salads: If your child is used to chopping they could chop up the fruit themselves. Just grab whatever you have in the fruit bowl and your child can squeeze citrus fruit over the top to keep the fruit fresh.

Crackers: You can top a cracker with almost anything. I've always got crackers in the cupboard and then the children grab what we have to make toppings. Things like fruit, cheese, spreads, vegetables and even butter and sprinkles on a treat day.

Cocktail and kebab sticks: For some reason, if food is on a stick children are much more likely to eat it. Provide a mix of favourite foods and one or two new foods and encourage your child to make a food kebab.

Baking

You might need to plan ahead for this or you might have already created a stock of dry mix. Baking is a really sustainable activity as you can buy the majority of the ingredients packaged in paper and will not need to buy premade alternatives packaged in plastic.

Play-Ready

Create a baking box with flour, sugar, baking powder and anything else you might need. Alternatively use the recipes at the back of this book to create a stock of dry mix.

Five quick ideas

Oat biscuits (p.123): All you have to do is add the wet ingredients and bake. You will be cutting down on waste from packaging as well as providing sustainable play for your child.

Soda bread (p.124): This is a great recipe if, like me, you're not a pro-baker. There's no proving to do so it's quick and easy. Make it playful by providing flavour ingredients for your child to add in.

Oatmeal muffins (p.125): Add the wet ingredients and bake as you need them. If you make a big batch you can freeze some and when you want to eat them just take them out of the freezer. Allow an hour or so for them to defrost at room temperature.

Cupcakes (p.126): Once your cupcakes are cool your child can decorate them with fruit or sweet treats.

Cereal cakes: Melt chocolate and add your favourite cereal. If you want a really sweet treat your child could add mini marshmallows. Put them in cupcake cases and pop in the fridge to eat later.

Fruit blends

I'm not a huge fan of kitchen appliances but our blender probably gets used more than the oven. Fruit, vegetables, pancake mix, milkshakes, you name it, the kids have probably blended it.

Play-Ready
If you already have a blender, you're good to go. If you haven't, you don't need a massive blender with ten different functions. Find a small, easy to use blender with a separate cup and blade so your child can fill the cup and you can operate it.

Five quick ideas
Fruit smoothie: Grab what you have in the fruit bowl or plan a trip out to your local farm shop and encourage your child to think about the flavours that will go well together.

Fruit milkshake: Milk and (some) fruits go so well together. Take this opportunity to talk about buying fruit without packaging. Take some reusable cotton bags to your local supermarket or farm shop and choose some fruit to blend with milk.

Fruit and vegetable smoothie: This is a great way to get picky eaters to engage with unfamiliar food. Be adventurous, it's amazing what children will eat when they are involved in the prep.

Fruit lollies: Use up any left over smoothie by freezing it, either in a mould or you can use a mug with a stick in. Put a cupcake case over the top of the mug, stick a lolly stick through. The case stops the stick from moving around and when your child comes to eat the lolly the case will catch any drips.

Frozen fruit and yogurt: A really fun and quick way to make frozen yogurt is to blend frozen fruit and yogurt together. If you want to be super sustainable you could forage for berries, freeze them and make your own yogurt from milk.

Food art

One way that I've tackled the waste associated with art and craft activities is to plan for creative time with food. The children can get creative and when the activity is over they can eat what they have made. If you provide packaging free foods like fruit, vegetables and fresh bread then your activity will be waste free.

Play-Ready
As I mentioned earlier, to be play-ready you simply need a good range of foods in the cupboard.

Five quick ideas
Popcorn and fruit: Lay out a selection of fruit and popcorn and your child can make a picture with it.

Fruit and vegetable selection: You can get an incredible amount of colour from fruits and vegetables so this is a wonderful way to excite the senses, play sustainably and creatively. If your child is able to chop soft fruits and vegetables then get them involved in the preparation. If not you can prepare the food and have it ready on the table. Encourage your child to look at the colours and shapes and make a picture with them.

Toast, cutters and spreads: if you have some cookie cutters your child can use them to cut toast and then decorate them with spreads such as peanut butter, jam, marmalade, chocolate spread and honey. It's like painting with food and you don't have find a place to store it when they're finished.

Cocktail sticks and tinfoil: Make spiky animals or aliens using tinfoil rolled into a ball and cocktail sticks. Decorate with fruit, vegetables, sweets or berries and eat.

Grated/ribbons of food: If your child is able to use kitchen tools safely they can help you with the preparation. Ribbons and grated food make beautiful pictures. Carrot ribbons can be swirls and grated food can be shaped.

Breakfast

Breakfast on a school day in my house consists of either throwing something on the table, such as cereal and milk or, on a good day, having time to put some toast on. If you're lucky enough to have a bit more time on your hands, make breakfast time playful and fun.

Play-Ready
Create a breakfast box with basic ingredients such as oats, cereal, nuts and dried fruit. Have a good stock of the raw ingredients needed for things like pancakes and waffles as well as fresh fruit and yogurt.

Five quick ideas
Pancakes: Scotch pancakes are always a winner in our house and I find them much easier to get right than a crepe. Use the recipe at the back of this this book (p.127) to make a dry mix and then add milk and egg when you're ready to cook. Fruit, spreads and cutters work well with pancakes. Your child could play by making a pancake tower.

Yogurt and fruit jars: My children love making these for breakfast. Lay out some ingredients on the table, give your child a clean jam jar and they can layer fruit, yogurt, honey and oats or granola. They love seeing the layers form and eating it afterwards.

Toast or waffle faces: Challenge your child to make a face on their toast or waffle. Use dried fruit, fresh fruit and grated ingredients for the hair.

Breakfast kebabs: Again, if it's on a stick they'll eat it. Your child can layer fruit, toast, waffles and drizzle honey over the top.

Tinfoil toast: Cut tinfoil shapes and encourage your child to make a picture or pattern with it on top of a piece of bread. Grill the bread and reveal the pattern after it has cooled.

Lunch

For my picky eaters, lunchtime has always been the best time to introduce new foods. As long as the children weren't tired or grumpy, I could subtly include a few unfamiliar foods with the familiar and by making the meal feel like play, they were much more likely to eat.

Play-Ready
Think ahead. If you want to include pasta, rice or couscous make sure you have prepped the night before. Think about foods that make a good base like bread, wraps, rice cakes, crackers and cooled cooked grains, pasta and pulses. You can build on these with fruit, vegetables, cheese, spreads and cold meat.

Five quick ideas
Wraps: Get your child to make their own wrap with whatever you have in the fridge or cupboard. It could be sweet, savoury or both.

Shape sandwiches: Your child can use cutters to cut their sandwiches into shapes.

Pasta salad: Brighten up a pasta dish by adding fruit, vegetables, olives or cheese.

Wrap pizza: My children love these and they're so easy to do. Give your child a wrap and a tube of garlic and tomato paste. The squeezing is fantastic for muscle development and when they have spread the tomato and garlic on their pizza they can top it with their favourite foods and some cheese.

Savoury cupcakes: Put a selection of cupcake cases on the table along with crackers, cheese, cut up fruit and vegetables. Encourage you child to assemble the food inside the case to make a 'savoury cupcake.' This activity if fun, hands-on and will distract a picky eater.

Dinner

Dinnertime can be playful too but there should also be opportunities for your child to sit nicely with a plate of food and use their knife and fork to eat it. If seven days a week of sitting nicely at the table is too much (and when children are under three it usually is) plan for fun, buffet style and finger food dining.

Play-Ready

Plan your week and set aside a couple of days where you might introduce a playful, hands-on meal.

Five quick ideas

Nachos: Really fun hands-on dinner. Heat up some nachos and cheese and lay out the food you want your child to eat with it.

Pizza night: Make your own French bread pizza or make your own dough base. Pizza dough feels lovely and children really enjoy kneading it. It's a sensory experience and encourages creativity.

Fajitas: There are so many options with fajitas. You could make them meaty, vegetarian, vegan or even sweet if you wanted them for dessert. When children think there's competition for food they come straight to the table and engage straight away. There's also a element of choice with a meal like this and when children feel like they have a bit of control they are more likely to eat.

Tacos: Just like a fajita meal, you can lay the food on the table and allow a bit of freedom and choice. You may not want every meal to be like this (we need to know our children are getting a balanced diet) but once or twice a week is fine.

Party food: This sounds really unhealthy but it can be super healthy, it's up to you. If you call it a 'party' and lay the food out on the table (buffet style) your child is in control of what they put on their plate and they are much more likely to eat.

Dessert

Dessert is usually my way of bribing the children to finish their dinner. By creating playful desserts that allow your child to be involved in the making, it gives them something to look forward to after they've finished their main meal.

Play-Ready
Always have a good stock of fruit, yogurt, cereal, chocolate, honey, dried fruit and ice cream. You can easily combine these ingredients and make a huge range of desserts. Dessert doesn't have to be unhealthy; try to include as many fruit based desserts as possible.

Five quick ideas
Chocolate dip: Put a small cup on top of a big mug of warm water. Your child can put the chocolate inside the cup and wait for it to melt. Once melted, they can dip cut up fruit into the chocolate.

Ice cream factory: This is one of our Friday night treats. I lay out ice cream, caramel, strawberry sauce, broken up biscuits, marshmallows, chocolate for grating and so on. The possibilities are endless but try not to have too many heavily packaged ingredients; you could make it more sustainable and healthy by using fruit instead of sweets and make your own sauces. The children create their own ice-cream sundaes. If you have sundae glasses even better.

Pancakes: If you have any left over batter from breakfast, put it in the fridge to reuse or make the pancakes and keep them to warm up later. Pancakes can be topped with sweets, fruit or spreads and make a lovely dessert.

Cupcakes: At least twice a week I make time for the children to bake something. Use the cupcake recipe at the back of this book. You could either pre-make the cupcakes and your child can decorate one after dinner (freeze the rest to stop you from eating them all) or your child can help with the baking and decorating.

Fruit kebabs: Fruit kebabs are amazing for any time of day. This activity is fantastic for your child's fine motor control and allows them to be creative.

Natural environment Play

Natural environment Play

When you provide opportunities for your child to play outside, in the natural environment, you are adding an extra layer of sustainability to their play. When children play outside, it supports their wellbeing, helps them to develop physically and provides 'real' and memorable learning experiences.

Forest and woodland

The forest floor provides natural, sustainable resources for your child to use during play. The sights, colours, sounds and smells provide sensory stimulation; no prep needed.

Play-Ready
Plan. If you don't plan to go out it's easy to caught in a comfortable 'stay at home' routine. You don't have to out for the whole day, if your child is young a thirty-minute stroll in the woods might be enough.

Five quick ideas
Colour hunt: Cut four pieces of card into leaf shapes (you could use red, blue, green and brown) . Use a Stanley knife to carefully cut slots on each leaf shape. Challenge you child to find colour. If they find something red, for example, they can slot it into the red card and so on.

Mud monsters: If you're lucky enough to find a really muddy area, make piles of mud and decorate with sticks and leaves to make monsters.

Den building: If you have an area with low trees, take some blankets or a tarpaulin with you and create a den.

Listening games: When you are exploring the woods with your child encourage them to listen to the sounds around them. See if they can identify what is making the sound. Play 'Where are you? I'm here!' Get your child to close their eyes while you hide. They shout, 'Where are you?' and you reply, 'I'm here!' See if they can follow your voice to find you.

Woodland picnic: Make a day of it by packing a lunch, taking a blanket and having a picnic in the woods.

Beach

The beach provides open space, fresh air and natural resources. There's nowhere to hide so you can allow your child to run free and expend some energy.

Play-Ready
If you're planning a trip to the beach get a bag ready in the morning with towel, spare clothes and something to sit on. I hardly ever take resources with me, the beach provides sand, shells, pebbles, seaweed and rock pools; more than enough to keep the kids entertained.

Five quick ideas
Holes: Children love digging holes. It might be two holes connected together by a tunnel or one big hole to hide in. Holes can become imaginary boats or aeroplanes.

Tidal pools: If you live near a beach with big tides like we do and you know the tide is rising, position yourself a few metres from the shore and dig a tidal pool. When it's finished, if there's time, dig a channel so the water can reach the pool before the tide takes it away.

Rock pooling: You don't need lots of resources to explore rock pools. Gentle hands and sharp eyes will do. Remind your child to be respectful, place rocks back in the position they found them and if they pick up a creature they must also put it back where they found it.

Sand angels: The beach is the perfect place to create sand angels. Find some dry sand and get wriggling. Your child can decorate their angle with seaweed and shells when they've finished.

Treasure hunt: Take a reusable cotton bag to the beach with you and collect sea glass, shells and anything else beautiful.

Meadow

Meadows are wonderful places to find insects and interesting plants. Like the beach, the wide-open space allows your child to run around safely.

Play-Ready
I think it's useful to take a small bag with a magnifying glass, bug identification sheet and binoculars but you could plan a resource free meadow walk.

Five quick ideas
Hide and seek: If your meadow has long grass you can play a game of hide and seek or 'Where are you? I'm here!'

Bug identification: Meadows are teeming with insects and bugs. See how many you can find and if your child can identify them. Talk about their identifying features such as legs, wings, antennae and colour.

Cloud spotting: Make your own cloud spotter by making a card frame, draw the different types of cloud on it and write the names. Lay down on the floor, look up to sky and see if you can name the clouds. If there are not many different types you can look at the clouds and talk about what they look like (dragons, rabbits and whatever your child imagines).

Collect fallen plants: Anything on the ground can be collected and taken home for temporary art or craft.

Kites: Make a kite to fly in the meadow. This is a great time to talk about sustainability and renewable energy sources.

Caves

The first thing you need to ensure before exploring a local cave is that it is safe. We have a beach (the children call it 'cave beach') and its caves are safe to explore but you have to make sure the tide is falling. Caves are fantastic for sensory development. They are dark, damp and sound echoes as you move into them.

Play-Ready
If you are planning a coastal cave adventure check the tide table and make sure the area you are going to is safe.

Five quick ideas
Cave drawing: Take some charcoal or other natural mark making material and make some temporary cave drawings.

Story telling: Caves are really atmospheric and a great place to tell a scary story (make sure your child is not emotionally sensitive before you do this). If you have a sensitive child perhaps they can make up a story about a friendly bear.

Exploring echoes: My children will grab any opportunity to shout and inside a cave is definitely the place to do it. Encourage them to shout a word and then be very quiet to hear the echo of their voice.

Reflection: Take a torch with you and see if you can find any reflective surfaces in the cave.

Shadow puppets: Use your torch to make shadow puppets with your hands. Tell a story while you act it out.

Garden

If you're lucky enough to have space outside use it as much as you can. Create areas to attract wildlife, children will play with bugs longer than any shop bought toy.

Play-Ready

My play-ready garden has a mud kitchen, bug hotel and a toad house as well as a variety of plants for the children to take cuttings from. Your garden has to be your own but I do think children engage more with nature than they do with plastic garden accessories. Nature is ever changing so it's really difficult for children to become disengaged. The plants and natural elements in your garden won't fade or go mouldy, they'll move through cycles of growth and your child can enjoy watching the garden change from one season to the next.

Five quick ideas

Mud kitchen: Set up an area for mud kitchen play. Your child can combine natural resources and engage in imaginative play.

Bug hotel: Create a bug hotel. It can be really simple, such as a pile of branches, leaves and small logs or you could go a step further and create a woodwork project.

Cuttings: A great way to practise scissor control away from craft activities is to allow your child to take cuttings. They can use the cuttings in mud kitchen play or for temporary art.

Treasure hunt: Hide some 'treasure' around the garden and make a map to help your child find it. The treasure could be sea glass, chocolates or toys, it doesn't matter what you use. Afterwards, your child might like to hide some treasure for you to find and draw a map to help you.

Wind chimes: Reuse old metal by creating wind chimes. All you need is string and anything metal that can be tied on. For example old keys, screws, metal washers or screws. Once everything is tied on, find a stick and tie all the metal objects to it.

Growing

If you don't have a garden, it doesn't mean you can't grow anything. Some plants thrive inside and if you choose small and low maintenance plants your child is more likely to keep looking after them.

Play-Ready

Decide on your growing schedule in January and get stocked up. Seeds, compost (or create your own compost) and a little tin watering can for your child is enough. You don't need plastic tubs; reuse tins, jars, toilet roll tubes and anything made of cardboard to start seeds off.

Five quick ideas

Sunflower fort: Sunflowers grow incredibly well. If you like the idea of a willow dome but don't have the resources for it, you can create a similar effect with sunflowers. Plant them in a circle with an opening or, for a secret den, plant them in a spiral so you can't see inside.

Vegetable patch: Create a vegetable patch and use it as an opportunity for sustainable talk. Help your child to understand how vegetables grown at home are free from packaging and pesticides.

Herb garden: If you don't have room in your garden for a vegetable patch you can grow herbs inside. Use a sunny windowsill and you can talk about the benefits of growing your own food with your child.

Fairy/dinosaur grass forest: If you have a tray, bucket or old planter you can grow grass inside it to use during small world play. The grass becomes a magical place for fairies or a wild and dangerous forest for dinosaurs.

Bean in a jar: If you want to teach your child about growth and don't have a garden you can grow a bean in a jar. Put damp cotton balls or paper towel in your jar and place the bean down the side, between the glass and the cloth. Your child can watch the root and shoot break through and grow. You could read 'Jack and the Beanstalk' alongside this activity.

Zero Waste Play

Zero Waste Play

Very often the most fun I have with my children is when we're interacting with the resources we already have or when the house is tidy, the resources are away and we just have each other as entertainment. Never underestimate the power of laughter, talk and game play!

Dressing up

Dressing up doesn't need to be an expensive activity. You can use handmade resources and items of clothing from your own wardrobe.

Play-Ready
Collect pre-loved clothes and make your own dressing up box or just let your children loose on your own wardrobe and see what costumes they can make.

Five quick ideas
Pre-loved box: Sometimes you'll come across clothes that are too worn to wear outside or too extravagant. Clothes like these can be used to make a pre-loved dressing up box. Visit your local charity shop and you might find some costume jewellery or handbags to add to the box.

Handmade box: One of your craft activities could be to make things like capes, belts or hats for the dressing up box.

Jewellery: Again, look for pre-loved items rather than buying new. Dressing up clothes for children are often plastic and nylon heavy. I think it's much nicer to give them a quality pre-loved necklace rather than a new plastic alternative.

Masks: During craft time you could make some masks for your dressing up box. If you have some favourite books to go alongside your box, your child could make masks and role-play to the story.

Mum and dad's wardrobe: This works particularly well if your child is engaging in imaginative play and are in role as a parent. All of my children have enjoyed wearing dresses, heels, shirts (great for doctor play) and ties. There might be a bit of tidying up to do afterwards but it's definitely worth it.

Games

Game play is incredibly important for children. It helps them learn to negotiate, collaborate, follow rules, be a 'good winner' and cope with losing. Playing games together as a family helps you connect and games can be completely resource free.

Play-Ready
Make some game-play lolly sticks. Write a resource free game on each lolly stick and when you want some fun collaborative game play you can pick a stick at random.

Five quick ideas
Charades: This doesn't have to be movies and books, if your child is very young they could act out animals instead.

Sleeping mummy/sleeping daddy: This is a great game if you're exhausted and need a rest. Find a comfortable place, lay down and ask your child to find five objects to place carefully on your tummy or legs. Pretend to be asleep (or actually fall asleep) and your child has to tiptoe into the room and try to collect the objects without waking you up.

Hide and seek: Fantastic for collaboration, counting and patience. Your child can hide while you count and vice versa. When children are very young they usually pop out and show you where they are so you might need to model the game for them or get another adult to hide with them and show them what to do.

Hide the teddy: Some children don't like to hide or feel scared if the adult in charge is 'gone'. In this case you can hide a toy instead. Use 'hot and cold' to help them if they can't find the teddy. The younger the child the more obvious your hiding place will need to be. If they are very young you might even need to hide it clear view to start with.

Corners: You can use this game to consolidate number, phonic or colour learning. Make two sets of four cards. It might be two sets of numbers 1-4 or two sets of four colours. Put one set in a bag so you can't see them. With the other set, place one card in each corner of the room. Your child/children sit in the middle of the room to start with and when you say 'go' they pick a corner to sit in. Take a card from the bag and if it matches the corner your child is in, they are out. If you have more than one child, the players who are out have to sit in the middle or they can help you pull the next card out.

Dancing

Most children love to dance. The younger they are, usually, the less inhibited they are. Dancing is physical, it helps children to unwind (or sometimes wind up) and all you need is a clear space and some music.

Play-Ready
Add dancing games to your jar of lolly sticks and when you want some resource free play your child can pick a lolly stick at random.

Five quick ideas
Just dance: Put some music on and dance. Choose different styles and see if your child adapts their movements to the music.

Musical bumps: Your child can pick their favourite songs and when the music stops they have to sit down. This game is fantastic for listening skills.

Musical statues: The same as above but when the music stops your child has to stand still.

Learn a routine: Go online and search for 'kids dance tutorials'. Find your favourite songs and learn how to dance and follow a simple routine.

Make up a dance: Once your child has learnt a few steps they can put them together and make up their own dance. Once they have practised it, they can perform it to you.

Races

In the garden, on the beach or even in the house; races are a fun way to teach children how to channel their competitive spirit. As well as this, children need to learn how to deal with losing and it's another opportunity to play sustainably.

Play-Ready
You don't need resources but think about what you already have that your child could use during a race.

Five quick ideas
Book race: Fantastic for concentration and balance. This is a slow race. Your child can balance a book on their head and see if they can get from one side of the room to the other without dropping it. You could turn this into an investigation. Try and find out which books are easiest to balance.

Tidy up race: If you have a reluctant tidier, make tidy up time fun by turning it into a race. It doesn't have to be a race against a person, it might be a race against the clock or a song; challenge your child to tidy up the puzzles before the song ends.

Sock and spoon: Simply roll up a sock and balance it on a spoon. Mark out a start and finish point and create some simple rules such as what to do when you drop the sock and so on.

Obstacle course: This is a fun and creative race. It works best outside but you could create a soft obstacle course with sofa cushions and beanbags for balancing inside. Challenge your child to create an obstacle course. It might have a balancing challenge, something to jump over and something to crawl under. Once they have created their course, time them to see how quickly they can complete it.

Movement race: Choose any movement. It might be hopping, skipping, jumping, crawling or moving like an animal. When you have decided on the movement have a race. This is sustainable and supports physical development as your child engages different muscles as they move.

Singing

Singing is expressive, it supports acquisition of language and is something you can do together.

Play-Ready
Have some songbooks or go online. Remember to sing in the car or while waiting for something, singing is a fun way to help time pass quicker.

Five quick ideas
Name that tune: Hum or whistle a tune and see if your child can guess what it is.

Action songs: If you know some actions songs, teach them to your child otherwise use books and videos online to help.

Karaoke: Don't worry if you don't have a karaoke machine, most songs will have a karaoke version online. This is a great activity if you have a reluctant reader. My eldest needs a push to read his schoolbook but is always happy to read and sing songs online.

Sing and sign: Learn the signs to your child's favourite nursery rhyme or song. By making the activity physical as well as oral it helps young children to remember the words and teaches them about the needs of others.

Learning songs: Days of the week, months of they year, continents, you name it, they'll be a song about it online. I always remember my Italian lessons at school. Our teacher would make us sing to help us learn verbs and I can still remember the songs now (can't remember what I did yesterday though). Songs can really help cement learning so get online and make your screen time count.

Final Thoughts

I hope that you feel empowered to build some sustainable play into your current routines and teach your child how to make planet conscious choices. Remember that most of us can't be 'zero waste' all of the time; sometimes play involves consumption of resources. There will be times when a child needs a particular resource that might conflict with the ideals of sustainability but if most of our play is low waste and some of our play is zero waste, collectively this will have a huge impact. Remember that an evening spent prepping dough or creating dry mix for baking will set you up for weeks of play. Taking a bag with you on walks means that you can provide your child with free, natural and sustainable resources for play and having play-ready areas in your home means that your child can be independent. I hope my ideas spark your imagination and help you to create some sustainable play ideas too.

Play Dough Recipe

<u>Dry ingredients</u>
20g Salt
40g Flour
½ teaspoon of cream of tartar
½ teaspoon of corn flour
A pinch of powdered food colouring (optional but it looks amazing when they add water and the colour changes)

<u>Wet ingredients</u>
5ml oil
35ml hot water
For best results use boiling water but do not allow your child to add the water in this case.

<u>Method</u>
Combine your dry ingredients and store in a labelled jam jar. When you are ready to make the dough, simply pour the ingredients into a bowl, add the oil and then the water slowly, stirring as you go. Knead the dough for 5 minutes and leave it to rest for 10 minutes after that get playing. Store in an airtight container. If you haven't played with the dough for a while you may start to see salt crystals. Give the dough a good massage and the salt will recombine with the dough.

Additions
Essences
Rice for texture
Scented flowers
Dried herbs
Aromatic Spices (mild)

Health and Safety
Check all ingredients for allergens
Always supervise your child
Do not eat
Do not use essential oils
Do not allow your child access to boiling water

Disposal
Dispose with your food waste

Oat Biscuit Recipe

<u>Dry ingredients</u>
150g plain flour
2 teaspoons of baking powder
150g porridge oats
100g golden caster sugar

<u>Wet ingredients</u>
150g melted butter
2 tablespoons of honey
4 tablespoons of milk

<u>Method</u>
Combine the dry ingredients and store in a labelled jam jar. When you are ready to make the biscuits heat the oven to 160 degrees C. Pour the dry ingredients into a bowl, add the wet ingredients and stir well. Your child can add extra ingredients for flavour. Use a spoon to scoop the mixture, place it on a baking sheet (you can make large biscuits or lots of small ones) and pat down with your hand. Bake for 10-15 minutes. Cool on a wire rack before eating.

<u>Flavour ingredients</u>
Chocolate chips
Coconut
Dried fruit
Chopped nuts

Soda Bread Recipe

Dry ingredients
250g plain flour
A pinch of salt
½ teaspoon bicarbonate of soda

Wet ingredients
200ml full fat milk
1 tablespoon of lemon
1 teaspoon of honey

Method
Combine your dry ingredients and store in a labelled jam jar. When you are ready to make the bread, heat the oven to 356 degrees F/180 degrees C. Pour the dry ingredients into a bowl and add flavour ingredients. To make buttermilk, combine the milk and lemon juice. Wait about 10 minutes before adding the honey. Combine the wet and dry ingredients and stir with a knife. Shape the dough and put it on a floured baking tray. Bake for 40 minutes and leave to cool before serving.

Flavour ingredients
Herbs
Cheese
Olives
Sundried tomatoes

Banana Oatmeal Muffin Recipe

Dry ingredients
120g plain flour
200g oats
75g golden caster sugar
3 teaspoons of baking powder

Wet ingredients
2 mashed bananas
2 eggs
3 tablespoons of sunflower oil
250ml milk

Method
Combine the dry ingredients and store in a labelled jam jar. When you are ready to make the muffins heat the oven to 180 degrees C. Pour the dry ingredients into a bowl, add the wet ingredients and stir well. Your child can add extra ingredients for flavour. Share the batter between twelve muffin cases and bake for 20-25 minutes. Cool on a wire rack before eating.

Flavour ingredients
Chocolate chips
Coconut
Dried fruit and seeds
Chopped nuts

Easy Cupcake Recipe

Dry ingredients
125g unsalted butter (softened)
125g golden caster sugar
125g self-raising flour
2 medium eggs
2 Tablespoons of milk
A pinch of salt

Method
Heat the oven to 190 degrees C. Cream the butter and sugar together. Add the flour, eggs, milk and salt. Whisk until smooth. Share the mixture between twelve cupcake cases and bake for 15-20 minutes. Cool on a wire rack before eating.

Toppings
Icing
Sprinkles
Grated chocolate
Caramel
Crushed biscuit
Edible flowers
Chocolate chips
Coconut
Dried fruit
Fresh fruit
Chopped nuts

Scotch Pancake Recipe

<u>Dry ingredients</u>
175g self-raising flour
40g golden caster sugar
1 egg
200ml milk

<u>Method</u>
Combine all the ingredients and stir well. Oil a large frying pan and either make one large pancake or 3-4 small pancakes. When you start to see little holes in the pancake it's time to turn it over. Keep any leftover batter in the fridge, you can use it for dessert pancakes or breakfast the following day.

Sustainable Shopping List Essentials

Below is a list of sustainable essentials to keep in your kitchen cupboard. If you're always well stocked, you will always be 'play-ready'. Many of these resources can be used across a range of activities.

Newspaper
Flavoured tea
Plain flour
Salt
Cornflour
Liquid and powdered food colour
Oil
Rice
Cream of tartare
Essences
Dry herbs
Mild spices
Dried lavender
Peppercorns
Lentils
Bicarbonate of soda
Oats
Cereal
Chocolate
Seeds